Song Of The Midnight Fox

Eileen Sheehan

for Jane + Barbara
best wishes
Eileen Sheehan

ᴔ DOGHOUSE

Song Of The Midnight Fox
is published by
DOGHOUSE
P.O. Box 312
Tralee G.P.O.
Co. Kerry
Ireland
email: doghouse312@eircom.net

May, 2004
December 2004, Second Impression

ISBN 0-9546487-1-4

Edited for DOGHOUSE by Noel King

Doghouse acknowledge the assistance of Kerry Group plc.

Thanks also to Tuatha Chiarraí

Cover design: Fintan Wall
Cover illustration: Anna O'Byrne
Printed by Tralee Printing Works, Denny Street, Tralee

for my father and mother

Michael Flynn and Chrissie Barrett

Acknowledgements are due to the editors of the following in which many of these poems, or versions of them, were first published:

Agenda; Books Ireland; Breacadh (Ed. Rosemary Canavan); The Cork Literary Review (Ed. Sheila O'Hagan); The Cúirt Journal; Cúm (Ed. Moya Cannon); Equinox; I Am of Kerry (Ed. Valerie O'Sullivan); Heart of Kerry (Ed. Noel King); The Kerry Anthology (Ed. Gabriel Fitzmaurice);The Mermaid's Purse (Ed. Emma Cooke); MUZE (Ed. Stella Bellem / Anne-Marie Glasheen); Podium III (Ed. Noel King); Poetry Ireland Review; The Rialto; The Shop; Source; Southword; Staple; The Stinging Fly; The Stony Thursday Book; The Waterford Review; Words (Ed. Marion Moynihan).

Thanks to Radio Kerry where some of these poems have been broadcast.

Three Little Words and *Song* have been set to music and recorded by Japanese based band Cannery Row. Thanks to Colin O'Sullivan (vocals) and Bill Blizzard (music).

Thanks also to *The Fia Rua Writers' Group*. A very special thank you to John W. Sexton and Margaret O'Shea.

Thanks to Niall MacMonagle and to Killarney250 for the launch of this book.

Contents

Angel

He said, *I am old and*
everything has a bitter
taint and besides
I have only these oddments
to offer; things broken,
unfinished, unused and I'm not even
sure why it is that I've
kept them so long.

But she saw how his body
radiated light and he carried
not just a jumble of wheels,
coils, springs, but the very
ones she'd been needing to
mend the faltering
mechanisms of her heart.

And his eyes were pure
as a child's

        and she knew

from that moment on
she was his
entirely

Trick Of The Light

Take that poem I wrote when I was five,
about a rabbit, one we had at home:
teacher read it out in class. I recall it
line for line. I know now that, as poems go
it wasn't great, it was really only verse.
As for the rabbit, he's long dead of course.
I can't recall his name but his sleek fur
was velvet like the dress I wore to mass.
The dress was red we also had a pig.
His name was Wiggser-Waggser. I wrote
no lines for him but poked inside his belly
to fish stored pennies out. I treasured him
but have no memories of the rabbit. Yet
the poem I wrote about him still lies curled
inside a tin in my parents' empty house.
I never wore that velvet dress. Velvet
came much later and the dress was green.
It matched my eyes and my eyes are green
but only

        in a certain slant of light.

Stranded

Light falls on a woman walking the edge
of the sea. Behind her the tied-up swings
are mute and motionless. The tide has laid
its honest gifts at her feet; smoothed stones,
a shell, the clean skull of a bird. A band
of copper seaweed struggles in the foam.

She stares in a pool welled up through sand:
more herself than she has ever been;
her own face stares back, beautiful, obscene.

What The Old Woman Said

I will tell you this. There was a garden by the pump. Fallow land given me.
My father built flowerbeds. Offshoots of paths. Geometric patterns.
Cuttings. Bulbs from my mother. The texture of earth.
Stone. The smell of water. I could grow anything.

I will tell you this. There was a pond. Wrinkles of mud.
Pups that were drowned there. Dragged to the bank. Sackfuls slit open.
Way beyond saving. Names that I gave them. Returned to the water.
Each small splash. Spirals expanding. My own face rippling.

I will tell you this. There was a heron. Constant. Returning.
Stilt-leg. Growing above water. Curtain of willows.
Everything still. A crowning of feathers.
Inflections of music. Nothing was moving.

I will tell you this. There were meadows. Light. Nectar from clover.
More flowers than I could name. Armfuls I carried.
Stems that I split. Smelling of summer.
Chains on my neck. Ankles. The bones of my wrists. Knowing nothing.

I will tell you this. There was a boy. Eyes like the sky.
Eyes like my father's. Children imagined. Rooms that were borrowed.
Rooms that were painted. Stories invented.
Histories. Futures. We knew everything.

I will tell you this. There was a man. Veins under skin.
Bones. Barely there. His stuttered breathing.
Green light on a screen. Intermittent beeping.
False light. False music. Someone was dying.

I will tell you this. I had seen his face on the shroud.
Running and bleeding. Wounds on his hands.
Pictures on glass. Coloured and leaded.
Faces on statues. A cross through his heart. Light always fading.

I will tell you this. There was a room. White. A white plate on the table.
A man at the table. Notes in his voice. A tune that I knew.
Beauty in the movements of his face. His arms. Frisson of wings.
Touch   Touch me   But he already had. I had forgotten everything.

I will tell you this. Some days are unbearable. Horizontal planes.
Moment to moment. Each long tick. I have been lonely.
Last night; a dream of a heron. The span of his wings.
Sounding through air. *Listen   Listen   I am disappearing*

Two-And-A-Half Year Old

My see me in mommie's eyes,
can her see she in mine?

My see me in mommie's mirror,
my see my two eyes.

My can see in mirror eyes
two mes, side aside.

My see me in window.
My in hot oven door.

My vrooming in the cars in town,
Oh look, in mine cornflake spoon

My see me upside down.

My not in the clouds.
My gone? No,
When my big me fly. Look,

Down splashy puddle here
My see me up the sky.

Tadhg's Meadow

I stroll through flowers, weeds,
memories pouring through me
damp and soft as the meadow grass
where we ran, arms laden
with cuckoo flowers; and where we
paddled the forbidden
icy stream; forewarned of otters waiting
to clamp a young ankle
and grin at skin-burst, bone-crack;
then swish-slither off; vindicated.

And we were in and out between the ricks
sun-bare and brown as our arms and legs;
our toenails cropped and sharp as the mowbar grass.

And we were round as barrels
quickrolling down the flower-flattened,
grassy, grasshopper way.

And we were wind and rain as we ran,
our hair mad as the grass,
high as our knees
and wet as our upturned faces,
headlong down the flying hill.

Where we turned,
explorers now,
to reach the summit.

And children then,
squelching home
to steam and drip before the fire.

Ring

My arm moved in a smooth
high arc through the dark night air
as I cast my sister's ring
from my hand. It landed soundlessly
in grass that moved like water.

There had been some trouble in the house
and dad was angry, really angry,
when my sister came home late;
and mother, who was always fired with talk,
was strangely silent. I hid inside
the pages of a book and understood
not one part of what went on.

Later, while they slept, the darkness
called me out. I stole the ring
because the boy she liked
had given it. The warm grass
welcomed it and murmured
some mysterious thing;
my own breasts already coiled
underneath my elastic skin.

three little words

Down by the river
Written on a fish
Are three little words
  wish wish wish

Down by the river
Written on a fern
Are three little words
  turn turn turn

Down by the river
Written on a stone
Are three little words
  gone gone gone

Down by the river
Written on a briar
Are three little words
  liar liar liar

Down by the river
Written on a leaf
Are three little words
  thief thief thief

Down by the river
Written by my hand
Are three little words
  sand sand sand

Down by the river
Written on my tongue
Are three little words
   alone alone alone

Carer

It's only ten o'clock
and already I've been called
a thundering cunt
at least three times.

Her curses are washing me clean,
clean as the smiles of my son
who is entering language so joyously
as he sits miscounting his toes.

The birds at the feeder outside
all seem interchangeable,
I can't keep account
of their flitters and squabbles,
their jostling for more.

And tonight outside of
this very same window
the darkness will move
with its various faces
and the stars,
which are countless, look down
on a speck of a woman
who somehow is standing
outside of herself
and no longer keeps score.

Bryan Says

the moon
is a white banana.

Bryan says
the grass
is waving goodbye.

Bryan says
there's a ghost
behind the squirting board.

Bryan says
we can't go yet
I gotfor my machinegun.

Bryan says
there's an X
under his bed.

Bryan says
there's a smell in his nose
get it out.

Bryan says
fireworks makes trees grow ·
in the sky.

Bryan says
we can't go yet
I gotfor my superhero ninjaguy.

Bryan says
elephants
is not kangaroos.

Bryan says
the moon is a plate
for his dinner.

Bryan says
Bryan's curls
are really, really yawney.

Bryan says
we can't go yet
I gotfor my sister.

Bryan says
he's not a gobbeldygook
he's just a Bryan

and you know,
he may be right.

Guardian

My father,
a most gentle man,

fed the leavings of the table
to nesting crows
that screamed and whirled
in a nearby stand of trees.

From a branch of sycamore
that overhung
his newly-planted drills,
he suspended
by its gnarled legs
one dead crow;

for weeks
the wind-jigged carcass
swung there
in a crazy parody of flight.

My father,
a most gentle man,

appeasing the dark gods,
their appetite
for sustenance
for blood.

Demented

A dead woman
lives in our house
but she won't lie down.

She keeps on
chipping away
at the ware in my kitchen;
unsettling the children,
calling me names.

Yet we keep her around
old Lady Lear
hunched under madness,
slopping her food
like a child,
rummaging through rooms
for a past that evades her,
but she won't lie down.

Still we keep her around
for those times
when the calm evening light
falls soft on her face
as she sleeps by the fire

the dead image
of my mother.

People Ask

People ask
Does she still know you?

I answer *Yes*
she knows me still.

    She calls me
         head in a book girl
         different to the rest girl
         wherever you were got girl.

Daughter.

She calls me daughter.

I answer *Yes,*
but who are you?

Bloodline

(i)
My face turned away from you
I was paring your corn, seeing only
the flecks of dead skin
that littered the floor.

Your voice droning on
with old stories, old grudges,
old wounds being reopened:
I had heard them before.

Then you mentioned a name,
a name not my father's:
*this was long before
I knew him*, you said.

Your voice was the voice of
the girl that you were;
you were nobody's mother,
no hurts had been done
and no one had died.

And we laughed together as you told me
how your mother lit the air around you
in the morning, when she found
the tell-tale signs of evergreen hedging
snagged in your long, red hair.

(ii)
She was kept
from her mother's funeral
by some green, festering hurt.

The coffin was lowered
in her absence
and a door in her heart
slammed shut.

(iii)
A darkened room
a narrow bed
a child afraid of sleep.

> The darkness clots, congeals
> to moving forms around her bed
>
> a line of faceless women
> a low hum sounding in their throats
>
> hands
> lift her
> lift her up and out
>
> higher than the ash tree in the garden
> higher than the house
> higher than the steeple in the nearby town
>
> hands
> ease her
> ease her down

A brightening room
a rumpled bed
a child wakes.

(iv)
With a switch of sally
you split my sister's face
cheek bone to jaw bone;

a gaping welt,
livid, white
as the naked bone of the twig:

a dark ribbon of blood erupts.

(v)

A child in a fevered bed
of tangled sheets;
heat, sweat,
a numbing cold.

For three days
you fed her soup
and sponged her down,

read stories filled
with perfect mothers
who always had to die;
stepmothers invariably nasty,
mirrors, woodsmen,
no end of tedious chores,
dragons, always slain
and always, always
the handsome prince
arriving just in time.

Common duties,
things that mothers do;
they were enough.
Enough to heal a child.

(vi)
Thread
Ribbon
Cord
Rope

A loop
A bow
A knot

A noose:

Stranglehold
of blood.

(vii)
A child wakes to a world turned red
red on the sheets
red on her thighs

and a wild anger
in her mother's eyes
toward her own dwindling blood.

(viii)

I dreamt that my heart unfolded
its blood-red wings and flew
out of the cage of my ribs
into this heavenly blue
you were waving to me from the garden
I was calling to you and you heard
Mother look, look, I am flying.
I am weightless as a bird.

(ix)
My ideal of love
is a bright illusion
a mirage that wavers
in arid heat

let go of it
and freedom happens

and so I turn
my naked eyes to you

child
woman
wife

red-muscled tunnel
that pushed me
screeching
into this light.

Old mother

I am your daughter
kneeling here

I pare your corn
I wash your feet.

In Defence Of My Dark Poems

He thinks
I can hook birds
out of the trees
at will,

haul kites
from the air,
order their ribbon tails
into precise syllables,

as if I had control of this.

Sometimes,
white eyed monsters
flounder to the surface.
Gulping creatures. Ugly.
Ugly babies.

Dreaming Snow White

If, while journeying through darkened woods
you stepped into a clearing
and found me stretched there dead
with all my hair spread out
my body white as camphor

would you raise the lid that held me
would you kiss me on the mouth
would your velvet tongue dislodge
the bite of poisoned apple from my throat

and would there be a white horse
his golden bridle gleaming
his breath like surging water

impatient to spirit us away
to some Happy-Ever-After

Piseóg

Today I was assailed
by the sulphurous stench
of rotting eggs.
It brought me back

it brought me back

to where I knelt beside my mother
in the garden, tugging weeds.
Her fingers stroked the crust of earth
and sank inside a putrid clutch
of buried eggs. She took a spade
and called up every curse she knew
as she sloughed the reeking slime
into a bucket.
              She poured it in
the steaming hole she'd dug
inside the dunghill, then scrubbed her hands
with water from the spout.
She blessed the fractured ground
with holy water and a scattering of salt.

Then hugged me to her fiercely, saying,
Remember this girleen. Remember this.

Lament

All the crosses you carved
In the bread that you baked,
In the end, could not save you

From the steel grey worm
That eats you
From the inside out:

Eats the names of the days
Events as they happen
The care that you took of your flowers

Eats the songs that you sang
The small things you wished for
Your laugh that could fill up the house

Eats the red from your hair
Your smoothness of skin
The spark that lived in your eyes.

I am trying to right it
Redress what is lost
Steal back your memory one cell at a time.

I loved what is lost of you
Must love what is left of you
Although some days I hate you

And some days I wish you could die,

But I wake in the night
Crying *Where has she gone to?*
And I fold like a child in the womb.

If I could I would save you,
Would mother you, mother,
Would suck you up into my womb

I would grow you again
Enrooting new memories
I would give you all new songs to sing.

I make poems for you mother,
Page after page piling up
As if this could save you,

Still you wake in the night
Crying *Nothing is ready, if anyone calls*
There won't be enough to go 'round.

I am trying to write it all down.
It is all that I know how to do,
To conjure with ink and with paper

These word spells that never can save you.
All I can offer are these,
Poor scratchings that only betray you.

New Decade

I was twenty nine
The first time my father
Took my arm for support
To walk the few yards
From my car
To his own front door.

After tea I drove home
With my grave thoughts,
Discomfited, as if
Some stranger was lodged
In the back seat, gloating.

Last Rites

There should have been a scapegoat on the night
he did not die: the one who made the calls,
he 's taken bad, you'd better come.

                        And so
they gathered in the house they'd grown from, like
strangers fogbound for the night. The sisters made
the tea and when they had it done they found
the table crazily laid: all knives, no spoons.
One noticed how her teeth left little shapes,
like crescents, on the thickly buttered bread.

By turns they sat with him.The youngest held
his papery hand, and once, he smiled.
But still his breathing laboured on. His teeth
still grinning from the glass beside the bed,
long after the priest had gone.

lines from the closing act

He woke and said
*I am dreaming
and you've all grown strangely strange.*
But to tell you the truth
they didn't know what to say so they said
No, nothing has changed.

He closed his eyes and said
*I see it all so clearly now
and your faces are white and still.*
But to tell you the truth
they were laughing, they said
It's time you took your next pill.

They opened their eyes and he said
*You dreamt me while you were sleeping
but I am much older than that.*
But to tell you the truth
he looked younger, they said
You look different without your old hat.

He slept and he said
*I smell flowers and jasmine,
somewhere a long way off.*
But to tell you the truth
they smelled nothing that sweet, said
What do you take for that cough?

They slept and he said
I am ready for road.
I'll be gone, just say the word.
But to tell you the truth
they cried in their sleep, said
Don't leave us. But he never heard.

Letter To Canberra

What can I tell you?
The fish is defrosting on the countertop;
there is no end to the rain,
the sameness of the days is stifling and
after three years looking at our father's headstone
I noticed, just last Sunday,
they spelt the name of the townland wrong.

Strange that now, at thirty-four,
I resent your going. I waved you off
too young to see how I would grow
in need of a sister. I miss knowing
the tone of the squeak
your back door makes on closing;
the exact patina of the cracked cup
at the back of your press
that nobody throws out, everyone avoids.

Eclipsed

You ask for news, but can I tell as news
how a certain line has called inside my head
for three days now: I nearly missed the eclipse,
the way the sky grew dark mid-morning.
The clean rain came flowing down my window
unselfconscious as a child's tears.

                                Last night
my daughter dreamt a unicorn, she dreamt
herself as part of his bright landscape. Today
the waking world seems dull to her. She draws
a picture of a mother and a child
identical except for size. I tell her
that mother is a soft word for whispering,
an old word, a babe's first sound, a strong word
for sheltering by, a place to grow from.

My Daughter Gathers Leaves

You ran in the back door
past washer and drier
the cluttered old dresser
your father's black boots
your little feet racing
your voice all excited
to show me the treasures
you'd gleaned in your play
outside on the crisp autumn grass

your arms overspilling
with leaves you had gathered
your pockets poured more
in a stream on the tiles
your wellies were brimming
with fistfuls you'd stuffed there
your hair was embroidered
red, amber and gold

Look at me, I'm a tree
I'm a tree and I'm dancing
Look at me, I'm a tree
I'm a tree in the wind

I looked and I looked
and my kitchen went spinning
as a fountain of colour
flew out from your limbs.
I picked up your rhythm
your colours, your vision
could have spun there forever
with you in my arms
Little Tree.

Waking

I tiptoe the width of the landing
to check on my eldest child.

The curtains hanging open
the room half bright with streetlight,

he is sprawled
like any teenager
suddenly too broad
for his narrow bed,

his eyes in shadow,
his jawline shadowed
like a man's.

I go no further
than the door

for here in this dim room
sleeps a grief too deep
for a mother's healing kiss.

Yet he smiles in his sleep:
tossing ball on the green
with his two dead friends.

Until that Sunday morning
when it all came
crashing in,

death was a too-big jumper
stored on the highest shelf.

I have watched him,
tentatively
easing it on;
daily growing into it.

Midfield

You no longer look for my face
in the crowd at school matches.
Flicking your fringe,
you pretend not to notice
giggling girls on the sideline,
shouting your name.

I step back,
anonymous supporter,
allowing them better view.

You step back
pacing yourself
for a shot at goal.

Tomorrow, if the weather holds,
I'll wash your jersey.

Ego

When she doesn't want to make love
he says, *What's wrong?*
As if something must be.

She says, *There's nothing wrong.*

He says, *But there must be something wrong,*
the master, needing reasons.

She feels she should
have a note from her mother...

Dear Sir
would you please excuse my daughter from sex
the time of the month is not right
she's worried about the telephone bill
an earthquake rocked Tokyo tonight
she's afraid of waking the baby
Halley's Comet won't pass again for sixty seven years
she's afraid of making a baby
and the Dow Jones index showed
an unfavourable low at close of business
and you probably did it last night
two nights ago at the most...

He nudges her with his elbow,
Go on, you can tell me what's wrong.
Was it something I did? Something I said?

But there's nothing wrong, I keep telling you!

Deflated, he heaves towards the wall,
taking his questions and most of the blankets.

Freezing on the edge of the world
she knows that nothing is wrong,
for tonight she has learnt three things:

about ego,
the tug of the moon,
why women invented the headache.

Kiss

He came to me

his voice in my head
like a white flame licking

his hands through my hair
like a sweet breeze blooming

my name on his tongue
like a snowflake melting

his mouth on my mouth
like the warm earth yielding

Death is a seriously sexy man.

One For The Road

If I die before you
wear indigo at my funeral.

Have my friends recite rap poetry
from the back of the church
loud enough to make
my coffin tremble.

Place one broad hand
on the glowing wood
over the spot
where my left breast is

and I will liquify
under your touch
one last time.

For it is late spring
and I am tired;
of brave faces,
of love and anguish
being unspoken things.

Belief, Disbelief And Outright Lies

And what if, at the end of the whole
shebang, God is just an insurance salesman
with a pitch to die for; and the devil 's
a candle maker, self-employed and distributing
worldwide a range of her produce
that's branded in red, with a logo depictive
of Venus. And what would you say if I told you
that love is a man with a lawnmower
who pops his head in the window
to say, I present you a daisy I saved
from the blade, just for you, and I ask
in return, if you please, your unwavering gaze
on my arse while I finish this task.
So she gazed while he passed
and repassed by the patio door
and she thought, now, your arse in tight jeans
was the thing I loved first about you.
But we all have matured in the meantime
with children and pot-plants and attic conversion.
Despite this, she rushed out and kissed him
right there on the grass and so what if the neighbours
might stare, and the next day, being Sunday,
'tho' the grass was not finished, they rested.

The Second Law Of Thermodynamics

Ever since we bought
the emigrating preacher's
antique bed,
there's no stopping us.

This morning,
after the room stopped shaking,
we lay
flat out on the jumbled
patchwork spread,

This bed will be the death of us, he said.

vengeance is mine

God looked down
and for one brief second
saw inside
my womanheart
my womanmind:

God grew fearful;
resigned.

... worst thing could happen...

She scrunches her eyes, crosses her fingers,
repeats, repeats, *Worst thing, worst thing could happen
is*. Finding her cat squashed flat on the road?
No. No, not it. Not that but something close.
She had heard them whispering of the night
and the man found face down in the river

near where her father worked. So, the river
takes you. Just like that. She cried and her fingers
bled where she had bitten down and all night
people called saying, *Sorry this could happen*.
But the flowers smelled good, she held one, close
to her face as the black car parked on the road

outside the house, and people lined the road
and they were whispering, words like *river,
water, drowned, shame, a shame, no one close,
no one to save him*. And then her fingers
touched her mother's hand, *How did this happen?*
Her mother shook her head, *Not now*. That night

she saw his face and a voice called, *It's night
and cold, so cold*. She ran but the road
was crumbling where she stepped, *Can't happen,
can't happen*, and the pull of the river
was too strong and she was only small: fingers
far too weak to save him. She huddled close

to a tree and felt the spiteful air close
in around her as she fell towards sleep, *Night
is my blanket, my very own*. Her fingers
hurt real bad; she chanced a peek: on the road,
her father, home from his work on the river:
smiling like the resurrected Christ. *Happen*

*I might have a story for ye, things happen
ye know, if ye know how to look real close
under stones, places like that*. But, *Stupid River!*
was the only answer she gave. One night,
he died for real, but not until the road
was long behind him: beads lacing his fingers.

The road winds on regardless and the river
holds its stories close, fathers die at night,
children cross their fingers ... *worst thing could happen...
is...*

Knowledge

Having gazed too long
I learnt
the gods exact their vengeance still

snakes in my hair
these pig's teeth
insensible flesh.

Don't come here
with your bright shield

I will not crumble
in the face of that
a second time

there is nothing here
for you to kill
or love.

Nothing flows here.

Nothing grows
in my stone garden

only these
grotesque gnomes:

too late they moved
to shield their eyes
from the sight of me.

One deathly glance

another stupid hero
stands before me
petrified.

Genesis

While my brother was transcribing
the Latin names of medicines
into cloth-bound ledgers
in the office where he worked

and the Woodbine on my father's lip
burnt backwards
to a long, grey ash

she freed me
into my new element:
not a bit amazed
at being born.

My sisters were fetched back
from the neighbour's
down the road

the eldest who was nine
already planning
how she'd plait my hair
and paint my toenails pink

the other, who was four,
locked her great dark eyes on me
and swore revenge
on this boneless, mottled thing
who dared usurp her place
as youngest child.

I smiled and father said,
*Ssshh, an Angel 's passing
somewhere overhead.*

I remember none of this.

Song Of The Midnight Fox

I will come to you
in a cloak of darkness
on a sultry night
too warm for sleep

watch for the cloud of my breath
on your window,
for the whimper of nails
on the glass.

I will lead you
past the boundary of the garden
on a zig zag path
through moonlit fields.

I will guide you
to a secret place I know of
where a warm stream feeds
a shaded pool

and as you shake the moisture
from your body
I will land you safely back
inside your head.

And when you wake without me,

don't dismiss me as some creature
the darkness made you dream:
I am real as anything
you care to touch.

Step outside my love
inhale the morning;
you will catch
my lingering scent on the air.

Auntie Annie

I loved her for the feathers
that she wore entwined
in the silver coils
of her hair. I never cared
that the grown ups thought it odd
to weave her hair with speckled browns,
with black of crow and white of herring gull.

She was the oldest woman
I had ever seen; half afeared I'd peek
from behind my mother's floral skirt
for her shapeless mass
in black, fringed shawl
and dull grey dress.

But her face was white and soft
as yeasty dough. A crease
ran down one cheek as if
someone had once traced
a loving finger there
and ever since her skin
had held the mark; a secret
glimpsed at only when she smiled.

Her kitchen reeked
of smoke and seaweed
and was hung about with nets;
my dad at ease by the open fire
as she dished up tea
in blue-striped mugs
and chunks of griddle bread.

Her talk was mostly
of the sea. She knew
the vagaries of winds and tides,
the greed of water
when it swallows; its power to feed.
She held respect for nature's whims
for both her sons were fishermen.

Sunday visits to her house
would punctuate our summers;
and I still can feel,
in my outstretched arms,
the solid weight
of her parting gift, gleaming
under folds of rolled up paper:
an iridescent fish.

Setting Out

The unsteady sway of the boat
as it moved across grey water
had me gripping, with both hands,
to the wooden seat. I watched
the castle growing smaller
until it was only a dark smudge
receding into a widening view
of water, shoreline, trees. And the fear
left me on that stretch of open lake
as a light breeze drew back my hair
and the spray's touch was gentle
as your fingers tracing
the contours of my face. The boatman
joked that he had drowned no one
so far that morning. I thought of bones
embraced by water, caressed
by weeds; of swimmers who never
made it home. Below me I saw
a woman looking up
from another world. I knew
there were urgent stories
she had come to tell and I
was all attention; her face
flashing past the boat in a continuous reel
as we neared the island. I smiled
down at her. In the shallows
she disappeared. With the engine cut
there was only the idle slabber of water
against the boat; the knock,
knock of wood on stone. I stepped out

onto the pier; like that first time
stepping into your arms: safer
than anything I had known.

On The Island

We left the others, to walk the round
of the island. The path, in places, was
slick with mud. Grasses loomed
taller than ourselves; briars sneaked out
at every turn, snagging our feet. Weeks
of incessant rain had lent a lushness
to the place. And the sonic-boom we heard
might well have been real thunder
the way it drew our faces to the sky.

They talked of childhood games and fairy-tales,
boys they had courted, pranks and staying out
late. *I had been wishing for thunder,*
something to take the heaviness out of the air.
The sunshine when it came was unexpected,
welcome. We looped our jackets round our waists,
more surefooted now where the path was drier, steeper.
Through the trees we glimpsed beads of gold on the lake.

Tourists smiled a greeting as they passed us. Walking
down-hill through knee-high grass, stands of foxglove
marked our way like sentinels. *I would have you know*
of a dark haired child playing alone in the
meadow: fairy thimbles on every fingertip.
I would reveal the places in a field
a child might hide in. A stub of pencil in her pocket;
scraps of paper covered in her awkward scrawl.

Back in the shade of the abbey ruins we joined the others
for sandwiches, coffee steaming from a thermos flask.
There was talk of art and inspiration, of passion,
of the sheer hard graft. *I have found a heart*
I am at home in. I celebrate the light,
the dark, that shaped it. The abbey offered
bleached stones; herb Robert blossoming from every crack.
Roofless, windows gone. Arched doorways offered no impediment:
no boundaries. *No more boundaries.*

Field Trip

On a two-day spree
midges, hungry for blood, nip
everyone but me.

Some bugs prove more wise:
ten sceartáns convey me home,
attached to my thighs.

* Sceartáns: ticks

In This New Town

The weather here articulates itself
in no set order. Fruits swelling
out of season. Birds of brighter hue
than I am used to: some days I am blinded.

Neighbours grow used to the late hours
I keep, my pale face on their streets
in the mornings. Everyone knows me as
stranger. I only moved here that he might see

my face; that I might grow
to know his features. But I lose sight
of him on crowded streets where ivied walls
reveal, in raised calligraphy, a route

I map with my fingers. I know the park by
scent, by a tremble of grass; its
audible whispers. The mist off the river
clings to my face, my eyes. On

the far bank, my own small house
grows visible. The woman who lived there
before me allowed it all run wild. I struggle
to reclaim the raised beds, the network of pathways.

And I have coaxed a gravid stray with
milk-soaked bread; each day she comes closer.
But sky when it speaks tells me
I am not myself, not myself at all.

my father visits my dream

my father visits my dream
and death had not changed him
and his voice sounded
like it always had

you must stop
intoning my name
like a prayer, calling me
calling me back, I have no desire

to be there, you must stop
with your knockings
and rappings, stay out
stay out of my head

girleen can't you see that the living
have no business haunting
the dead and he laughed
the same kindly laugh

and I woke and death
had not changed him
except be was brighter
than he had ever been

and suddenly he was everywhere:
I had found him again

Homecoming

In her absence
the kitchen was ruled
by a man.

She returned
to find everything
orderly, neat:

all toys out of sight,
no ware needing washing,

even the dog
was folded away
in his place.

The whole room smelled
of canned roses. But then

she opened her case
and spewed out her wares:

dresses and knickers and books,
all manner of intimate things
recklessly flung across chairs.

And she laughed
at the look of dismay on his face
for the chaos she'd wrought, and declared,

*The poet 's come home,
is reclaiming her space.*

Tabby

just
to love him

for he has all of the
predator about him

disdains scraps,
traps sunlight in the
nap of his fur,
weaves his scent-trail
through other gardens,
unsheathes sharp claws,
winds three times round
the circle of himself,
is merciless

yet graces my nose with
one swift kiss,
arches his body
to my touch,
curls in my lap,
laps milk from the bowl,
croons his guttural
song for me

reflects the glow
of the moon in his eyes,
incises a moth with a
snap of his jaws,
draws darkness around him,
soundlessly vanishes

all nine lives
intact.

I Asked My Love

I asked my love to lie with me last night,
his face appeared unchanged, his smile the same:
this morning I rose early with the light.

At his approach I felt the air ignite,
he whispered softly: spoke my secret name.
I asked my love to lie with me last night.

He said my eyes seemed older, he was right:
only the dead remain immune to change.
This morning I rose early with the light.

His lips touched mine as in a holy rite,
his touch seared through me like a sacred flame.
I asked my love to lie with me last night.

I trembled as our breath became one breath.
He brought me to a place beyond all pain.
This morning I rose early with the light.

He went from me just as the sky grew bright.
I called my love. I called my love by name,
I asked my love to lie with me last night.
This morning I rose early with the light.

Evil Eye

She looked at me
and thought she saw
a witch
a bitch
a twister

I held her gaze
she thought she saw
a spell
a well
a power

I raised my arm
she thought she saw
a wand
a threat
a danger

but then, but then,
on her own skin
an itch
a rash
a blister

and when she looked
at me again, she saw
herself: my sister.

Fire

I fell asleep and dreamt
that as I slept
one glowing spark ignited
in a room downstairs
and instantly
my whole house
was licked by flame.

I woke up naked

the covers tossed aside,
my skin adorned
with shining jewels of sweat;

my house, my room, my bed
apparently unscorched:
my whole body
yearning, yearning.

Awakening

I have found it at last
this bright space inside me:
a place that was here all along.

Like a gate that swings open
on a vast, golden meadow,
like the warm breeze
that ushers me in.

Like a bird that takes flight
and soars to the heavens,
like the music that pours
from his throat.

Like a man in a dream
who whispers a secret
as he places a jewel
in your hands.

an elegy of sorts

for want of an ash-tray
I rest my cigarette
on this grey plate,
a remnant
from some depleted set,
now serving as candle-holder

the cigarette tip sizzles
as it hits a pat of wax

I inhale and taste the tallow
as red seeps down the paper
stains the filter

a last molten drop
from a crimson candle, lit
as votive for an injured cat

the cat now buried
in a sunny spot
by the back wall

a favoured place of his
for grooming

somewhere
there was a point to all of this
which now evades me

like that raw evening,
placing his still-warm body
in the grave, how everything
but the weeping
failed me

Song

Sing me a song mother sing me a song
I'm needing your voice in my head
the music inside me is silenced
the notes grown stilted and dead.

Sing me the song of the young man
who drowned in the lake at Coolfin.
Sing of the deep and false waters
that lured him and swallowed him in.

Sing of the woman who mourned him
of the vigil she kept on the shore
crying and calling her lost love
of her yearning to hold him once more.

Sing me a song mother sing me a song
strike the air with notes that are true.
Prime me with words of your choosing
that I may sing my songs for you.

Birthday Poem

A day so perfect
there is nothing that I want
except to lie here
with this sunlight
warming my skin
'til the whole world is spinning
and I'm spinning within it

and I'm back

where a man with dark hair,
waist-deep in the river,
is checking his watch
and counting the minutes to home

and not far away is a woman
who steps into the yard
as she shakes out her apron,
her red hair aflame in the sun.

And soon he is home
and he smells of the river
and her kitchen is smelling of bread;
there's a meal that they share
and no one is counting.

And now they are sleeping.

They don't know my name
or the least thing about me.
They don't even know
I am here. I am here,
I am something nestled inside her:
my mother. A pattern just formed
a space newly filled. Finally,
finally, it is all making sense.

Maybe none of it happened
like this: I am writing a myth.
As I stand to go back in the house
the grass is sprinkled with buttercups,
daisies. Swallows are claiming
the air. My son is building
a castle from sand. My daughter
turns perfect cartwheels
the full width of the garden.